About the Author

Shannon Ryan is a twenty-seven-year-old writer and artist living in rural County Wexford, Ireland. Having been fortunate to spend a childhood surrounded by woodland, a passion for nature weaves its way into her work. She is most at home painting, writing, reading poetry, and long beach walks.

Elephant

Shannon Ryan

Elephant

Olympia Publishers
London

www.olympiapublishers.com
OLYMPIA PAPERBACK EDITION

Copyright © Shannon Ryan 2024

The right of Shannon Ryan to be identified as author of
this work has been asserted in accordance with sections 77 and 78 of
the Copyright, Designs and Patents Act 1988.

All Rights Reserved

No reproduction, copy or transmission of this publication
may be made without written permission.
No paragraph of this publication may be reproduced,
copied or transmitted save with the written permission of the publisher,
or in accordance with the provisions
of the Copyright Act 1956 (as amended).

Any person who commits any unauthorised act in relation to
this publication may be liable to criminal
prosecution and civil claims for damage.

A CIP catalogue record for this title is
available from the British Library.

ISBN: 978-1-80439-145-7

This is a work of fiction.
Names, characters, places and incidents originate from the writer's
imagination. Any resemblance to actual persons, living or dead, is
purely coincidental.

First Published in 2024

Olympia Publishers
Tallis House
2 Tallis Street
London
EC4Y 0AB

Printed in Great Britain

Dedication

For Mum, your spine astounds me, thank you for being our *Elephant*.

We are more like the animals then we remember

My mother would think that there is nothing to repay

When I think I am indebted to her
For bearing me long after birth
For sheltering from a manmade storm

I think she is the vital
Everlasting maternal Elephant
Weather-beaten and constant

Pillars of stone that cradle the young

And the red sand is kicked up

She wears tones of the earth
Her bones are made of clay

She wipes my boots
And harbours my wonder

She's there when I go home quietly
Peeling in our single block insulated kitchen

And I feel bad

Other times my dinner is ready
Presenting on the table that has known the kneading of her hands

My Elephant has looked after me again

Thank you for believing in the
Shores of me
Soul of me
Shades of me
Specter of me

How I lean into your tide

The Elephant looks after our beloved collie Milligan
She wipes him too

His eyes as they secrete old age in a brown/red stream
Most days gently with cotton wool
And a white ceramic dish for the lukewarm water

My mother digs at the ground and puts flowers in her path

She cuts my hair and tells me to keep my head down
And tilt regularly
She shapes my face with my hair and pulls at the ends
Where the knots congregate and have stubborn meetings

My Elephant pats me down and burns the knots in the fire

Elephant wears horse printed scarves and silver ball earrings
that smell like the bottom of her handbag
My Elephant has tissues that smell like the red dirt of home

She carries a spare watch in the handbag inside a plastic pill bag

Elephant wears layers of fleeces like an unwashed onion with terracotta jeans
She layers these over the bed

My Elephant's eyes are faded green
Sometimes watery under a fan of brown tinted lashes
Frames the bones of a mother's face

She asks me if I have washed my mouth with salt
Then says keep rinsing

I think she has given me her cold hands and sensitive teeth

She is the mountain that holds up the sky

My mother's eyes are gentle like grass
She pushed us to grow and bend towards the light
The earth was home and mud pies could be made from it

She arranged our lives with green fingers, carefully

We were brought into life with a bomb in our house

The bomb aged
We aged quicker
Feeling the barbs with every year

Those years were as supple as the trees we climbed in
Our Elephant walked slowly with us, showing us the paths to take
The same ones she had planted flowers in

I lived in that wood when I could feel the bomb twitching
I think that's why elephants are so big; they can brace for impact
They pad the innocent

The bomb had grey hair in the wedding album and used to make apple tarts with flour on the kitchen table
He would pile breadcrumb volcanoes and flood the valley with milk. We stopped eating those.

I remember those little prayers I used to say to myself on the other side of the sitting room door
Hoping that when I went through the Bomb wouldn't say anything I worried about the noise I would make

The hallway was another valley the Bomb rolled around at night It had doors to the children
He talked as he paced

When the sickness came, he was thin of life
He slept a sallow sleep
But then again he was always sick
Always tired
Always bloated
Always threatened
Always unmaking

The bomb mellowed but dormant bombs are still capable
At times and how could I have forgotten so soon that you
were like a hound on a moor? I would forget this, a brief
visit back would remind me to retreat
How could I have forgotten so soon?

Not long before the bomb died my phone rang. It was the hospital; I was familiar with the number now. His temperature had gone up. Maybe I could go and see him? But I couldn't it hurt too much and I needed to protect myself from his instability. I had practiced this protection and natured it. It's the hardest thing to break, like the hide of an elephant. I feel my heart is hurt anyway.

I went to see him a few days later. Bomb was in his own room now. Contained. All the walls in the world couldn't do that. He said the nurses had been talking about me, that I didn't care to visit sooner. That hurt me too. I remember three days before you died you said you were disappointed in me and that I didn't love you. These were the last words you said to me.

He always had ancient hair
Like it had been shocked by life
Having three children instead of a wall full of paper plans
They would have been easier to handle
Easier to mend

He could have put blue and red stickers on our wings instead
and thrown us around when the wind was just right

I remember the smell of the green washing up liquid in the glass he would use to clean the elastic bands to clamp the wings with

The Elephant was more fragile than all of those planes thinner than the paper and she snapped like one of his rubber bands
A snap that went through the children
Through the folding of clothes

I remember the day before the first snap because she went around cleaning all the door handles even though the ceramic already shone
One of the handles had a pink rose on it

The Elephant wiped away all of her nerves until there were none left and the ambulance came and took the mother to hospital
The children didn't understand
I only knew I was upset by my runny nose
And my sister's arm around my shoulder

There was no tissue so I used my red trousers, making two lines in the fabric

The Elephant's grace, sanctuary, wholeness
Vanished into the hospital on a hill and emptied out the home
Until there was nothing left but children with oven pies for dinner

The bomb was an unusual home maker because bombs aren't meant to be soft and wash your clothes

Bombs eat on there own at 1 o'clock and watch the news 3 times a day

The Elephant, our earth's foundations
She strides around on the great red dirt Compacting our ground
Our footing

We lived our childhood through shades of green
Faded like her eyes in the Summer

I have elephant eyes but darker not yet faded by a thousand days under the red sun

She has amassed six jars of French jam in the cupboard now
primed for Summer sponges

The damp of the cave's floor goes up through the bones of the Elephant
She has a pair of shoes for every room

The bomb always had the biggest white socks in the world on until he would move about for food or traveling the hall. Huge socks went with giant runners that went out once a week to the supermarket

She used to wear brown tartan shirts
Brown shoes with a short heel were polished by something in a plastic bag

My brother got his dark hair from our Elephant

You kept us mended with a graceful thing that moved
unseen through the hours of the day

I remember sugar sandwiches for my lunch
I remember rainbow coats made by your mother worn to be passed on

The love of an Elephant is an immense thing
It fills you up until you believe you are enough by being yourself

Elephants have masses of skin that warm with the sun and tan like those jeans you wear

Sometimes I see you in the face of strangers,
In their padded coats
In their enormous white socks and grey hair
I think I have your thin hair
Will it grey as quickly?

In rounded stomachs bloated by medication and feelings of not coping
I have to check in those faces that it's not you that I haven't missed something in missing you.

But you couldn't keep the young in your temper
It's like building on sand

To make it hurt less I will say I am still getting to know you even though you're not here. And how things could have been different if not for the bomb inside you.

Maybe there was goodness but it came up from the ground and sowed the field with waving cow parsley.

I remember those pill bottles stacked at your end of the table like chess pieces waiting to be moved but they never seemed to make you better

I remember when you took a turn and walked around the garden with your arms outstretched like one of your planes.

You would say there was a smell in your nose before you had a turn

I remember the light in your bedroom was always brown and the dent in the wall were you hit your head

I remember a dinner time when the Elephant wasn't there
and you fell down You were always falling
And we had to push the chairs away from your head.

I remember being on that train with you and the lost man who wandered onto the track in the night.

I remember screaming into my pillow when I didn't like the way you talked to me

I wish I could pull at the wrists of that child and save her
Take her to where the air was warmer.

Why did you die before you could see me live

We bobbed like corks in your storm

I remember when you smothered damp coal on the fires

I remember finding your glasses around the house like shredded skins

I remember wanting you to notice me and being terrified when you did.

Homes can be carried on the backs of elephants in ways that can't be strapped to bombs

Being disappointed by you just fits like craters on the moon

I remember you last words were pushed out by pain that's why they felt like spite

It's amazing how you can still be hurt by a wounded animal in hospital socks.

I remember you getting really sick
It was like watching an old steamer go down and all its noises with it.
How I thought you'd exist forever.

I remember you on your hands and knees when your body let you down.

After you were gone I deleted your texts in case I ever found myself going over them someday. I was protecting myself even then.

I know the wind seeded those trees you said you planted for us in our names.

I knew the particular stillness of the kitchen where you sat
by at night
Talking to someone I couldn't see

I know there was probably only butter in the fridge when you died.

I remember when numbers made sense to you
And you taught me how to count with the abacus sat by the table at night

I know those plastic flowers in the window called out to be real.

I remember the burning car
On the side of the road
The day I bought you a tin of sweet corn.

I know you lived to see if our Elephant would come back. I knew she wouldn't, all the trees sowed by the wind in the world wouldn't have been enough shelter.

I remember watching you and waiting for the
Plummeting
Descending
Collapsing
Rolling
Turning

When I was a child it was like your weather was changing and I had to be ready

I could never understand how you couldn't remember the trauma of your body like I did

How could you not remember the bruises

How could you not remember the stain on the floor
or the cushion under your head?
I can't ask you now.

You are sometimes to me just someone that I used to know
Someone on the edges of my life but related.

But that's the thing about a Bomb
You live on the fringe with them.

You made me feel like a couldn't take up space in the world

You made me fit inside a teaspoon so I wanted to drown you in a thimble
Let you know how much you broke my heart

Maybe I was a threat to you like the asteroid to the dinosaurs, I could wipe you out too.
What power I didn't know I had but I was a child and my feet were small.

And I ate worry until it lined my mouth.

Your father is not well she would say
Not well
Not well
Not well
Not well

Our Elephant's way of saying stay close and keep to the shores of the red sand.

Fathers are meant to be well built like bridges so you can walk across their backs. And reach the other side safely. But my bridge was wired.

I wanted to blame you for those wildfires
For turning our home into a shell.

For having to pick out the tweed jacket you wore in the coffin.

For when you were more interested in planes flying then your children growing.

I was born with wings
You just didn't see them

But I was a child and the only thing I knew was the nerves in my mouth

I remember saying goodnight to you in the coffin
To imagine you were sleeping was gentler than saying goodbye.

You died how you lived, addled

That is what made you so bewildered

And the threads of your thoughts so percarious

I remember you hooded eyes

And the stoop in your spine

I remember when we moved out and there no more glass on the floor
I could dance then.

I remember worrying if you'd ask where we lived now.
I remember thinking I didn't deserve to be this free
And that eventually you'd come and blow it all up
Like our happiness was tethered to your state of mind.

I've put so much energy into protecting myself I am still exhausted

If only you had been well made and not hounded by sickness

I wish I could take the parts of you that frightened me and ask you to explain them.

Perhaps then I could have gotten to know you as your daughter

I just got so tired of the tears
Falling off my face
Like little torrents.

You died in April
Just when the flowers started talking to each other.

I will grieve for you
I will grieve for my childhood
For the parts of myself I lost in being afraid
For not being able to reach you when you were sick
For not letting you close enough to love me

For the times I spent believing I had disappointed you
For the times I had convinced myself it was something I had done
Childhood shouldn't be about surviving
Childhood shouldn't be about defending

I am finding parts of myself I didn't think were worth saving

I don't know the difference between guilt and grief
They wear the same face

Guilt can make a hollow of you

I am still wrung out from trying to prove my worth

I wish I could ask you did you ever see me
Did I appear on your horizon?

Calling you Dad is unknown to me
But I will take your name out from under the shade
Dust you down
Air you out
Spread you under the sun

Until your name becomes easier to say

I grew up knowing you as 'Him' never as dad or a person

I can still hear the music that fell out of your hands
When you strummed the guitar

How your voice was followed by a moon shadow

You sat on the edge of the bed like it was the edge of a cliff
Sometimes you'd fall off

I wonder did you ever see your children as extensions of yourself or birds you gathered along the way?

Despite the scale of your havoc it hurts me to know that you will never meet my children. I will have to search for the good parts of you.
Like finding flowers in cut grass but they will have something honest of you even if it its only petals.

Elephants are a lot like the canopies of mango trees, shading the young

That's why our Elephant has so many wrinkles around her eyes
From folding away our worries

I watched you make the bed like the four ends of the duvet were the four corners of the earth

I hope I have elephant bones in me and I'll be able to nurture as you have

You stun me with how you coped
And how you are healing

Watching you put socks on the line is like watching clouds in the sky.

You worry about the trees lose their leaves
Will they be able to cope?
Will they be warm enough at night?

There is a bell where your heart should be.

You dread horse flies and air your socks with the hairdryer

If you ask about me I'll tell you about my mother
We are herd animals.

We are ends of the same string

If I have tusks is it because of you

If I listen more than I talk it is because of you

If my wrists are small it is because of you

If I wonder about shipwrecks on the seabed it is because of you

If I hold my hands out it is because of you

If I tend to flowers like lambs it is because of you

If the sun slips from the sky and rolls about on the floor like a tangerine it is
because you have gone quite.

If I find it sad that I can count the number of ladybirds I've seen on one hand it's because of you.

If I like carrot cake it's because you fed it to me from the womb

If I'd rather leave the weeds the way they are it's because of you

If I mourn over a fallen bee it is because of you
There little souls have so much work to do

If I ever fear the thought of letting someone down it is because of you

My Elephant put me inside a drawer for safe keeping

She knows the times when I feel this world too much

She knows my fault lines
My Elephant senses my fears like tremors going up through her feet.

You bathed our small bodies in bogs of salt
To preserve them for better days

Those dark circles under your eyes know
were all those years went like tree rings

Thank you for planting me so carefully in this world
In the soil you slept in

When the Bomb wasn't well you were the safest place to be

You tell me there is a song for every word
And I believe you

I've followed your Sun like sailors searching for the North star

A Sun that warmed the soil we made mudpies from

You cherished us like ferns about to billow

You are a Sun that ties up her hair when she's pacing

Lavender grows under the warmth of your rays

This has always been for you
Every word.

Your shadow is not cold to be under
It is basking
It is rapturous
It is enchanting
It is almighty

You toiled so that we can flourish under your Sun

I've always wanted to feel my belly harden and for someone to call me Mother so that I can tell them it's okay to feel like bruised fruit. Someday they have Elephant hide to heal them.

I want to see what a rounded tummy would like under my nose
When I can no longer see my feet but just assume they are shuffling us forward.

I will teach you child how to forgive yourself when someone else's rage frightens you.

I will tell you home is where brass bells ring and to always keep a tissue in your pocket.
I will wrap you up in rainbows just like I was.

I will find more ways to tell you I love you
More ways to hold you up.

I'll make fairy wings for you child
Out of coat hangers
Just like my mother did for me.

I will dress your brothers and sisters in your second-hand rainbows
I will tell you flowers never die because we can press them inside of books.

Clematis will sprout from your scalp and flow down your back

I will tell you it's okay to keep part of you just for yourself

I will press your hands into terracotta soil

You are as precious as Van Gough's Sunflowers my darling

I will embrace you so close me
Your skin will mellow

You have the potency to shake the sky

And the tenderness to tempt flowers to smile

I will give you green eyes to see the world through and plant the trees you play in You will see this garden you have inherited by being loved.

These pages have
Shocked me
Broken me
Worn me
Put me back together
Pulled memoires out of my soul
This is my pain
My truth
In the daylight
You have my heart in your hands
All I ask is it you put it softly next to yours
Have only gentle hands about you and you will heal
Thank you
Thank you
Thank you